W9-BBA-231

THE 2006
COMMEMORATIVE
STAMP
YEARBOOK

Other books available from the United States Postal Service:

The 2005 Commemorative Stamp Yearbook

The Postal Service Guide to U.S. Stamps—33rd Edition

THE 2006 COMMEMORATIVE STAMP YEARBOOK

UNITED STATES POSTAL SERVICE

An Imprint of HarperCollinsPublishers

 The U.S. Postal Service thanks DC Comics for its generous contributions
to the design theme of *The 2006 Commemorative Stamp Yearbook*.

HarperCollins books may be purchased for educational, business, or sales promotional use.
For information please write: Special Markets Department, HarperCollins Publishers,
10 East 53rd Street, New York, NY 10022.

Library of Congress Cataloging-in-Publication Data has been applied for.

ISBN-10: 0-06-114456-8
ISBN-13: 978-0-06-114456-1

06 07 08 09 10 ❖ 10 9 8 7 6 5 4 3 2 1

Contents

Americana in Miniature

For decades, artists have struggled with the challenge of the perfect comic book cover: a creative combination of illustration, cartooning, and storytelling that serves to invite readers to the latest adventures of their favorite characters. The challenge is great, and the artists often have felt as heroic as the characters they depicted. But turning the pages of this Yearbook, I see clearly that my comic-book artist friends must bow to the geniuses of an even smaller canvas: the postage stamp.

For 2006, the U.S. Postal Service celebrates the American tradition of personal accomplishment with stamps that commemorate historical figures like Benjamin Franklin, distinguished diplomats who followed him in one of his many careers, notables from the worlds of sports, entertainment, and literature—and, oh yes, the super heroes who've made American comics a worldwide phenomenon. Each has been honored on the precise but tiny space of a stamp, and our nation's finest artists, illustrators, and designers have made those stamps into fine artwork. Even the covers and illustrations that were selected for the DC Comics Super Heroes stamps needed to be carefully matched to the available space and high standards of the 2006 commemorative program.

Enjoy, then, this collection of Americana in miniature, along with the accompanying informative text. As you turn the pages, remember the incredible deeds of the people and events on the stamps . . . but also take a small moment to appreciate the accomplishments of the creative people who have captured those American heroes forever in art for your collection.

Paul Levitz
President & Publisher, DC Comics

Nearly seven decades after his *Detective Comics* debut, Batman appears this year on a U.S. stamp.

Black Heritage

Hattie McDaniel

After the Citizens' Stamp Advisory Committee selected Hattie McDaniel as the subject for a stamp, one of the first questions the designers needed to address was how to honor this talented woman without showing her in a demeaning role. As a black performer in Hollywood during the 1930s and 1940s, McDaniel had to play numerous stereotypical characters. Once conventional, these roles are now somewhat controversial. The design team wondered: Could they honor McDaniel without depicting her in her most famous role, as Mammy in *Gone With the Wind*?

As they explored McDaniel's career, a more complete portrait emerged. The design team discovered that she was more than a character actress; she was

ABOVE: Vivien Leigh and Hattie McDaniel in *Gone With the Wind*.

LEFT: A glamorous McDaniel on Oscar night in 1940.

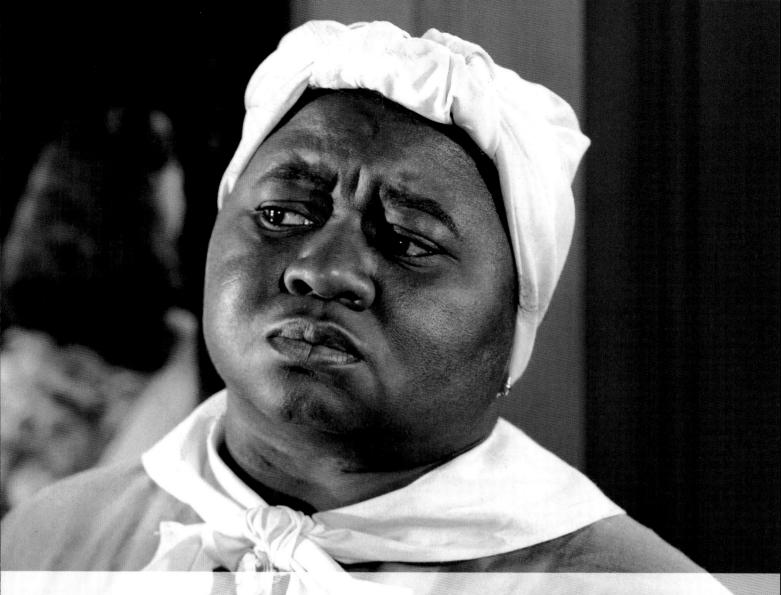

also a trailblazer for people of color in many areas of the performing arts, including vaudeville, radio, film, and even television. With this new stamp, featuring a portrait by Tim O'Brien, McDaniel takes her place as the 29th honoree in the Black Heritage series and an icon of strength and endurance for all Americans.

During her lifetime, McDaniel was often criticized for playing maids, slaves, and cooks. Having supported herself for many years as a maid, she knew what she was saying when she famously quipped, "I'd rather play a maid than be one." Recognized for adding nuance and complexity to many of her portrayals, she became a successful black actress despite the limited roles available to her.

In 1940, McDaniel received the Academy Award for Best Supporting Actress for her role in *Gone With the Wind,* becoming the first African American to win an Oscar. At the awards dinner at the Ambassador Hotel in Los Angeles, she wore an aqua blue evening dress and an ermine wrap accented by gardenias fastened with diamonds in her hair. Later, she said she was proud to have played a black woman "who was fearless, who cringed before no one, who did not talk in whispers, walk on tiptoe, who criticized a white woman's morals and who showed real emotion." The portrait on this stamp evokes McDaniel's moment of triumph, portraying her as the epitome of the glamorous movie star.

For the romantics among us, the Postal Service offers another eye-catching stamp celebrating love: two birds nesting together and colored blue to signify happiness and fulfillment.

Birds, which often symbolize freedom and wisdom, have long inspired artists, musicians, and poets. Shakespeare wrote about birds more often than any other poet, and William Wordsworth, ever inspired by nature, followed close behind, referring to 60 bird species in poems such as "O Nightingale!"

I heard a Stock-dove sing or say
His homely tale, this very day;
His voice was buried among trees,
Yet to be come at by the breeze:
He did not cease; but cooed—and cooed;
And somewhat pensively he wooed:
He sang of love, with quiet blending,
Slow to begin, and never ending;
Of serious faith, and inward glee;
That was the song—the song for me!

Designed by Craig Frazier, this new stamp captures the joy of nesting birds in early spring, the season most associated with new love.

Love: True Blue

Our Wedding

Central to the planning of any wedding celebration is the invitation. It's often the first glimpse the couple gives their friends and family of the day to come, but it's not only the words on the invitation that matter. Also important are the drape of ribbon, the texture of the paper, the colors—and, of course, the stamp.

Newly issued in 2006, the Our Wedding stamps feature elegant and elaborate Spencerian script, with flourishes and flowing loops reminiscent of the mid-19th century, when penmanship was an important skill. The white dove—a symbol of peace, love, and fidelity—completes the message.

Images of love associated with the dove have passed down through the ages. In Greek mythology, Aphrodite, the goddess of love, rode in a dove-drawn chariot, and legend holds that a dove flying overhead means that a woman's true love will soon be revealed. Another tradition claimed that if a couple must temporarily part, each person should keep one figure of a set of turtledoves to ensure that they return safely to one another and that true love will prevail.

2006 Olympic

Winter Games

Strength and fleetness of foot—these qualities, the ancient Greeks believed, were gifts from the Olympian gods. Centuries later, and in a wintry context the ancients never could have imagined, those timeless virtues prevailed again at the Olympic Winter Games, held from February 10 through 26 in Torino, Italy, and celebrated by the U.S. Postal Service with this stamp.

Prompted by a growing cadre of snow-sport enthusiasts, the Winter Olympic Games—initially called International Sports Week—were first held in 1924 at a small Alpine resort in Chamonix, France. That event attracted more than 250 athletes from 16 countries, spurring the International Olympic Committee to agree to stage winter games separately from summer competitions. After more than 80 years, the tradition thrives, and participation has increased tenfold. Excelling in such events as bobsledding, ice hockey, skating, and skiing, approximately 2,500 world-class athletes competed at Torino on the snow and ice to the delight of more than 1.5 million spectators.

This new stamp, which features an illustration of a downhill skier cutting into a turn at full speed, highlights an iconic moment in winter sports. Snow-skiing and modern equipment may have been inconceivable to the founders of the ancient Olympic Games, but the indomitable spirit of athletes—a word derived from the Greek for "prize-seekers"—remains universal. With this stamp, the Postal Service continues to honor the spirit of athleticism and international unity inspired by the Olympic Winter Games.

Favorite Children's Book Animals

After Royal Mail successfully issued the 2004 Entente Cordiale stamps with La Poste to celebrate 100 years of "friendly understanding" with France, the British postal service announced that additional joint issues with other countries were also likely. Excited by this prospect, the U.S. Postal Service immediately began to plan its first collaboration with Royal Mail.

Spearheading the effort on the American side was Terrence W. McCaffrey, Manager of Stamp Services for the U.S. Postal Service. He presented potential subjects to his counterparts at Royal Mail, while they consulted with their design review board. Once everyone had agreed to commemorate children's book animals, each side faced the tough task of deciding which characters to honor. In the process, they also needed to tackle questions of culture: How would the American public respond to animals from British literature? Likewise, would American characters translate for audiences in the United Kingdom?

In the end, both postal authorities agreed to share two characters— the Very Hungry Caterpillar and Maisy—and to work independently on the rest of the issuance. The results are two unique panes of stamps that celebrate cherished animals from children's books treasured by readers on both sides of the Atlantic.

Featuring what has become author and illustrator Eric Carle's signature style of painted tissue-paper collage, *The Very Hungry Caterpillar* (1969 and 1987) tells the story of one unusual caterpillar who eats his way through a variety of foods during the course of one week.

Children love the bold outlines, bright colors, and simplicity of the Maisy books created by author and illustrator Lucy Cousins.

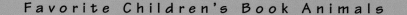

In *Maisy's ABC*—published in the United Kingdom in 1994 and in the U.S. in 1995—Cousins's mouse star helps bring the alphabet to life.

In 1941, Margret and H. A. Rey introduced American readers to a charming and mischievous monkey named Curious George, highlighting his light-hearted philosophy that the world is full of discoveries waiting to be made.

Whether painting the walls like a master or building an ambitious sand castle, Olivia is always the star of her own show. Published in 2000, *Olivia* won a Caldecott Honor the following year. It was author and illustrator Ian Falconer's first book to chronicle the energy and spunk of this loveable piglet heroine.

Maurice Sendak's *Where the Wild Things Are* won the Caldecott Medal in 1964 and instantly engages young children who readily identify with Max's feelings as they are carried away to an imaginary land of strange and fascinating creatures.

Illustrator Garth Williams gave form to Wilbur the pig, the inspiring and humble character in E. B. White's Newbery Honor-winning 1952 book *Charlotte's Web*. From his beloved friend Charlotte the spider, Wilbur learns about loyalty, bravery, and the joy of being alive.

Leo Lionni's use of torn paper collage and his celebration of nature, creativity, and kindness helped his 1967 book *Frederick* win a Caldecott Honor in 1968. During winter, Lionni's sensitive field mouse gathers together the colors and words that will make cold, dark days feel warm and bright.

First published in 1965 by Dr. Seuss, the pen name of Theodor Seuss Geisel, *Fox in Socks* features a playful and tricky red fox in bright blue socks. He leads beginning readers on a rollicking, tongue-twisting romp through a vibrant world of blue goo and cheese trees.

Quilts of Gee's Bend

The African-American women of Gee's Bend, Alabama—an isolated community located southwest of Selma on a bend in the Alabama River—began creating quilts for the practical purpose of keeping warm. "We only had heat in the living room," Loretta Pettway remembers, "and when you go out of that room you need cover."

After learning fundamental techniques from their mothers, grandmothers, and other female relations, each quilter must then find her own manner of expression. "I work it out," explains Annie Mae Young, "study the way to make it, get it to be right, kind of like working a puzzle." Infinite variations have made the quilts a source of pride and friendly competition for decades.

Until recently, necessity limited the quilters to fabric from everyday items such as flour sacks, old dresses, and worn-out work clothes. Noted for their unexpected color combinations and bold patterns, the quilts use stains, seams, and mended holes and tears to tell the story of Gee's Bend.

The quilts first gained national attention in the late 1960s, when some of the women from Gee's Bend joined with quilters in nearby communities to establish the Freedom Quilting Bee. Although the quilters enjoyed contracts with leading decorators and large retail stores, catering to popular tastes inhibited the improvisational techniques they valued so much. Many of the quilters soon left the cooperative, but they kept their traditions vibrant by continuing to make quilts for themselves and their loved ones. "I get pleasure from my quilts," says Essie Bendolph Pettway. "I enjoy seeing other people enjoying my work."

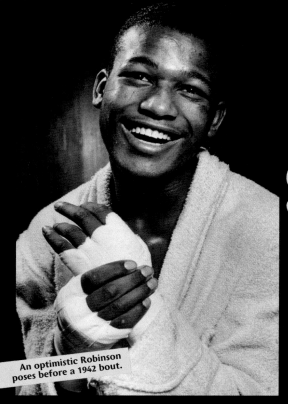

An optimistic Robinson poses before a 1942 bout.

Sugar Ray

"Fighter of the century": that was the verdict of a panel of experts assembled by the Associated Press in 1999. With this stamp, the U.S. Postal Service pays tribute to Sugar Ray Robinson, a six-time world-champion boxer and an icon of American sports.

In his prime, Robinson—born Walker Smith, Jr., in 1921—was virtually unbeatable in the ring. He reigned as the undefeated world welterweight champion from December 20, 1946, until February 14, 1951, when he won the world middleweight title for the first of five times. According to *The Ring Record Book,* he fought a total of 201 bouts, winning 174—109 of them by knockout—against only 19 losses, 6 draws, and 2 no contests. Of those 19 losses, 15 occurred after he was 35 years old, 10 came after he turned 40, and 5 happened during the last six months of his career when he was 44. No boxer could stop Robinson; heat exhaustion contributed to the only technical knockout he ever suffered.

Robinson's integrity and hard bargaining were as familiar in boxing circles as his impeccable and incomparable boxing style. He never once agreed to throw a fight, and he refused to fight for less money than he thought he was worth. His flamboyant personal style—he drove a Cadillac convertible painted flamingo pink especially for him—ensured his celebrity status outside the boxing world as well.

During and after his long boxing career, Robinson received numerous awards and honors: he won his first fighter of the year award from *The Ring* magazine in 1942 and his second in 1951, and he received the Edward J. Neil trophy for fighter of the year in 1950. He was ranked number one by the former editor of *The Ring* in the 1984 book *The 100 Greatest Boxers of All Time,* and in 1990—the year after he died—he was inducted into the International Boxing Hall of Fame.

Resembling a vintage fight poster from the 1940s and 1950s, this stamp features block lettering and a halftone image of Robinson created from a photographic portrait made during those peak fighting years. This portrait easily calls to mind the caption that accompanied Robinson's photo in 1951, when he appeared on the cover of *Time* magazine: "Sugar Ray Robinson: Rhythm in his feet and pleasure in his work."

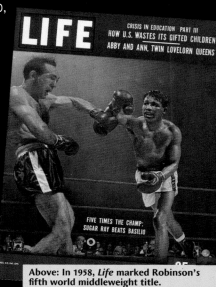

LIFE CRISIS IN EDUCATION PART III HOW U.S. WASTES ITS GIFTED CHILDREN ABBY AND ANN, TWIN LOVELORN QUEENS

FIVE TIMES THE CHAMP: SUGAR RAY BEATS BASILIO

Above: In 1958, *Life* marked Robinson's fifth world middleweight title.

Right: Robinson pounded Jake LaMotta on February 14, 1951.

Robinson poses with his famous Cadillac at two of his Harlem businesses.

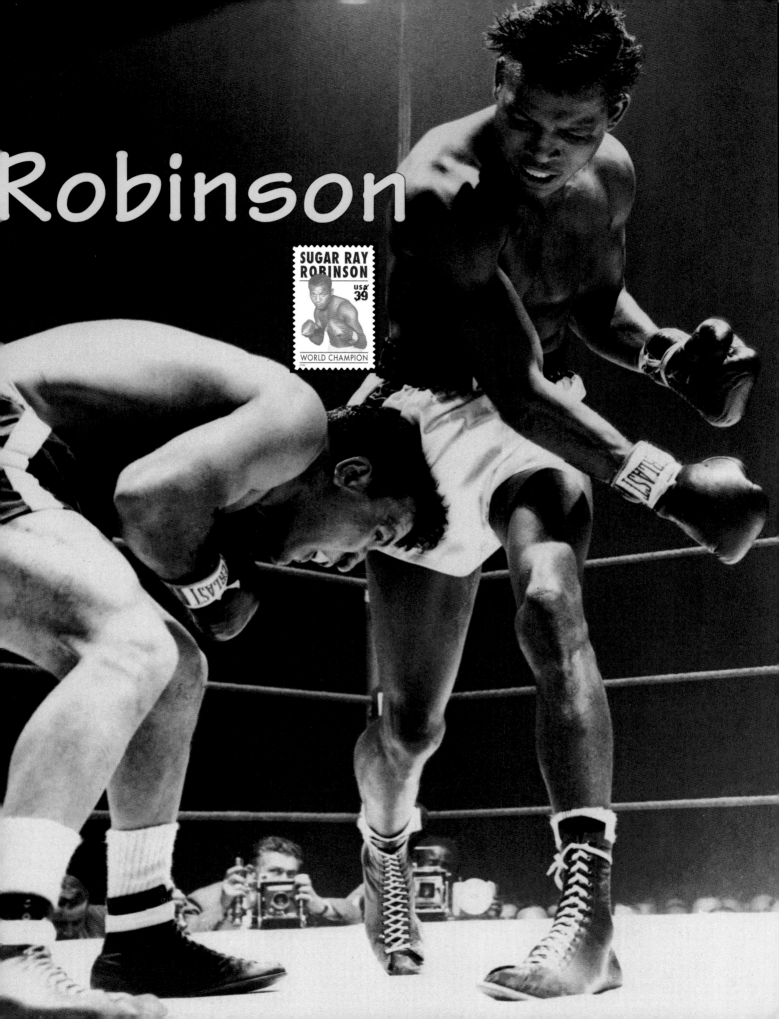

AMBER Alert

Recognizing that the loss of a child is devastating for family, friends, and communities, the Postal Service has long committed itself to the recovery of America's missing children.

Hoping to do their part, local post offices across the country faithfully display photographs of missing children, and for two decades, the Postal Service has also partnered with the largest targeted direct-mail company in the country. The program, "America's Looking for Its Missing Children," delivers postcards featuring photographs of missing children to 85 million homes each week. To date, it has helped recover more than 130 children.

In 2005, letter carriers took that idea a step further by participating in the search for a missing child and his baby-sitter while working their routes in East St. Louis, Illinois. Said local postal carrier Terrence Halliday: "If my son or daughter was missing, I would want people searching . . . we might get lucky when delivering packages by knocking on a door."

To further promote awareness of this issue, the AMBER Alert stamp honors a program dedicated to the rapid recovery of abducted children. Started in Texas, it was named for a nine-year-old girl who was kidnapped in 1996. Issued by law enforcement officers and broadcast over the Emergency Alert System, an AMBER Alert informs a community about an abduction as quickly as possible; speedy notification has proven critical to the recovery of kidnapped children.

AMBER Alerts have helped in the safe return of nearly 200 children, a positive message that artist Vivienne Flesher wanted to portray on this new stamp. Just as the program provides families with hope that they will recover their loved one, the stamp highlights the overwhelming joy of the reunited parent and child.

Literary Arts
Katherine Anne Porter

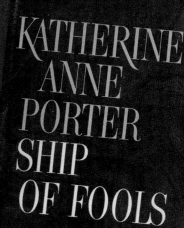

Strong-willed, intelligent, and gifted, Katherine Anne Porter is considered one of America's master prose stylists. Frequently drawing upon personal experience as inspiration, Porter believed that the artist's job was "to take these handfuls of confusion and disparate things, things that seem to be irreconcilable, and put them together in a frame to give them some kind of shape and meaning"—a goal she fulfilled admirably in her work.

Born Callie Russell Porter on May 15, 1890, in Indian Creek, Texas, Porter worked as a journalist in Texas and Colorado before moving to New York City in October 1919. There she began writing fiction and became acquainted with Mexican artists whose enthusiasm for their cultural heritage prompted her to travel several times to Mexico, where her story "Flowering Judas" was set. Her first short-story collection, also called *Flowering Judas,* won critical acclaim in 1930, and Porter went on to win the National Book Award and the Pulitzer Prize for fiction in 1966 for *The Collected Stories of Katherine Anne Porter.*

Today, Porter is also remembered for her only full-length novel, the 1962 bestseller *Ship of Fools,* which was based on a sea voyage she made from Veracruz, Mexico, to Bremerhaven, Germany, in 1931. By including a ship in the background of the stamp, artist Michael J. Deas alludes both to the novel and to Porter's assessment of her own life, which she called "this brave voyage." The artwork is based loosely on the S.S. *Werra,* a German ship that Porter described as "a tramp steamer disguised as a passenger boat."

For the portrait of Porter appearing in the foreground of the stamp, Deas used a photograph of the author taken in 1936 by photographer George Platt Lynes, who was also her friend. Considered something of a beauty, Porter went prematurely gray, and the stamp art captures her in her role as grande dame replete with haute couture dress and elegantly coiffed hair.

FACING PAGE: Porter photographed by George Platt Lynes around 1930.

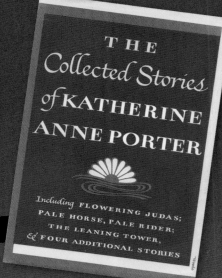

Benjamin Franklin

As a philatelist, art director Richard Sheaff knew that the 2006 Benjamin Franklin issuance would have to address several major aspects of Franklin's life and career: printer, postmaster, scientist, and statesman. Working with the Benjamin Franklin Tercentenary, a private nonprofit consortium that includes the American Philosophical Society, the Franklin Institute, the Library Company of Philadelphia, the Philadelphia Museum of Art, and the University of Pennsylvania, Sheaff had access to numerous artifacts, portraits, and ephemera. As a result, each of the four stamps is carefully layered with elements from Franklin's life and career.

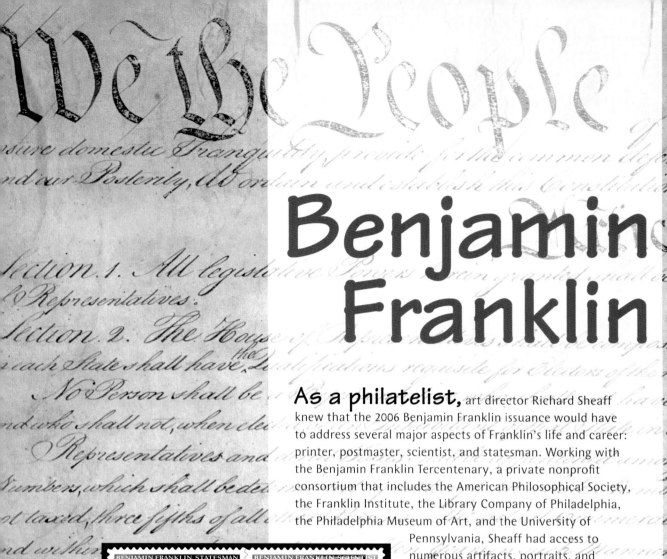

Franklin's successful businesses printed a wide range of materials, and he always identified himself with the business of printing. His last will and testament reads, "I, Benjamin Franklin, of Philadelphia, printer." The stamp honoring his work includes a copy of the *Pennsylvania Gazette* from 1729, the front cover of the 1733 edition of *Poor Richard's Almanack,* and a currency note printed by Franklin in 1760.

Throughout his life, Franklin remained intensely curious about natural phenomena such as electricity, meteorology, magnetism, and the Gulf Stream. The stamp art includes a page from his 1769 volume *Experiments and Observations on Electricity* depicting waterspouts and a "magic square," as well as a schematic drawing of his "three-wheeled clock," just some of his many "philosophical amusements."

Benjamin Franklin

For the stamp honoring Franklin the statesman, Sheaff chose a detail from John Trumbull's painting of the signing of the Declaration of Independence, Franklin's "Join or Die" cartoon—often considered the first American political cartoon—and the French side of the 1778 Treaty of Alliance with France, which Franklin negotiated and signed.

Given the wealth of materials, the most difficult of the four stamps was the one honoring Franklin for his work as a postmaster. Beginning with Franklin's own personal franking signature, "B. Free Franklin," Sheaff layered a colonial-era postmark and colonial postal cover on a late-18th-century painting of Franklin by Charles Wilson Peale, done after a portrait by David Martin.

In the immortal words of Franklin himself: "Resolve to perform what you ought; perform without fail what you resolve." With all due resolve, the U.S. Postal Service is proud to commemorate this unique American on the 300th anniversary of his birth.

Statesman

Postmaster

Printer

Scientist

WONDERS of America

Land of Superlatives

"America is a land of wonders," wrote French politician and traveler Alexis de Tocqueville, "in which everything is in constant motion and every change seems an improvement." With this stamp pane, the U.S. Postal Service proudly echoes the sentiments of de Tocqueville by highlighting 40 natural and man-made wonders: remarkable places, plants, animals, and structures selected from every region of the country.

Surveying the natural world, these stamps take collectors to such extraordinary places as Mammoth Cave in Kentucky, where more than 365 miles of passages have been explored and mapped, making it the longest known cave. Another stamp depicts Crater Lake in Oregon, the deepest lake in the country, with its bottom lying nearly 2,000 feet below the water's surface. Meanwhile, the largest canyon—the Grand Canyon—measures 277 miles long and, at its widest point, 15 miles across, earning it recognition as one of the "Seven Natural Wonders of the World."

The Wonders of America stamps also highlight several intriguing superlatives from the plant and animal world. These include the saguaro, the well-known symbol of the Southwest that can grow taller than a five-story

Place Stamp Here

ABOVE: A view of the Grand Canyon from Toroweap Point.

BELOW: A saguaro at Tonto National Forest in Arizona.

MAP OF THE
UNITED
STATES.

Scale 328 miles to an inch.

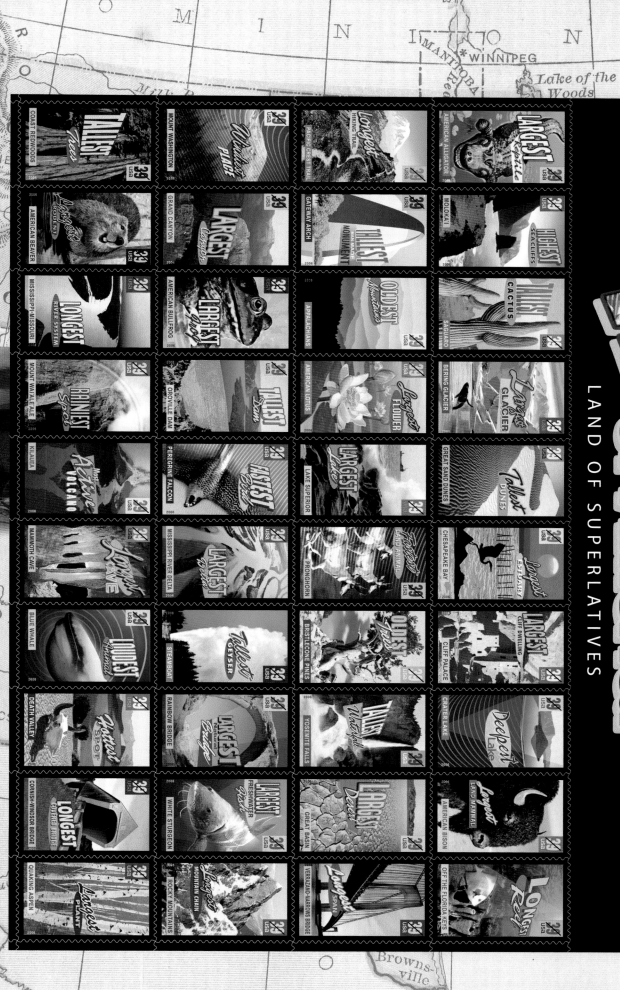

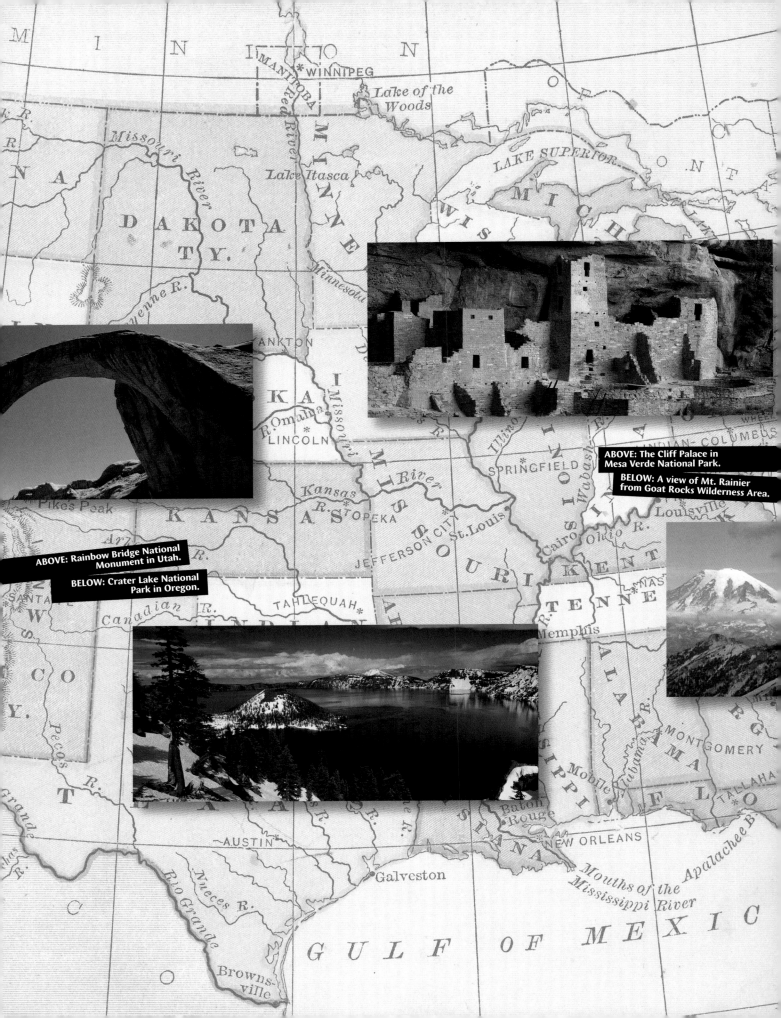

ABOVE: The Cliff Palace in Mesa Verde National Park.

BELOW: A view of Mt. Rainier from Goat Rocks Wilderness Area.

ABOVE: Rainbow Bridge National Monument in Utah.

BELOW: Crater Lake National Park in Oregon.

building. Another giant, the American lotus, grows in lakes, ponds, and streams in the eastern half of the country; its flower may reach ten inches in diameter. Swooping and slithering nearby are various record-holders from the animal kingdom, including the American alligator, which is the largest reptile in North America, and the peregrine falcon, the fastest bird in the world.

Numerous man-made wonders also make the list. These include the largest cliff dwelling, a centuries-old, multistory pueblo known today as Cliff Palace in southwestern Colorado, and the Gateway Arch in St. Louis, Missouri, the nation's tallest man-made monument. An East Coast wonder appears on the "Longest Span" stamp: The Verrazano-Narrows Bridge, which connects Brooklyn and Staten Island, has two 693-foot-tall towers that stand 4,260 feet apart.

Lonnie Busch, who illustrated the "Greetings From America" stamps in 2002, brings his playful sense of Americana to this new issuance. The information about each wonder was confirmed by multiple sources, but as is often the case, superlatives are subject to challenge—and to change. Different sources may use different criteria, while new discoveries and measurements made with more precise technology may cause old records to fall in the face of new information. Furthermore, in the case of man-made superlatives, it may be only a matter of time before a taller structure rises, a longer bridge is built, or a longer trail is completed. Until then, these stamps will serve as little monuments to grand and impressive things—and the quest for superlatives will continue to define our nation.

ABOVE: A sunny day at Yosemite National Park.

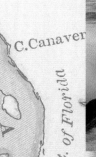

BELOW: Waves crash on the shore of Lake Superior.

ABOVE: A lovely view of the Verrazano-Narrows Bridge.

Washington 2006:

World Philatelic Exhibition

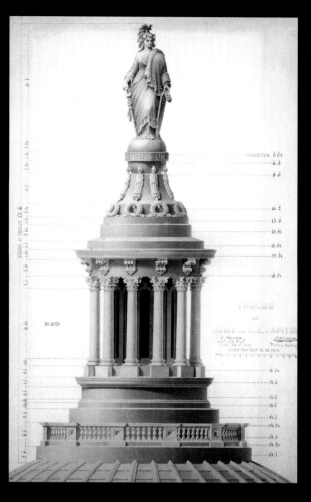

For eight days in 2006,

thousands of philatelists gathered in Washington, D.C., for the World Philatelic Exhibition. From May 27 through June 3, visitors viewed special exhibitions and attended meetings, workshops, and lectures. They shopped at the bourse—the philatelic name for a marketplace—and competed for prizes, all the while enjoying the best their hobby has to offer.

World Philatelic Exhibitions are international events held under the patronage of the Fédération Internationale de Philatélie (FIP). In general, these exhibitions are held at least annually, drawing thousands of stamp collectors and others interested in philately to host cities around the world. This year's focus on Washington offered a unique opportunity for the Postal Service to issue this souvenir sheet featuring reproductions of three stamps that depict well-known sights, issued in their original denominations and printed using the original dies created in 1923 by engravers at the Bureau of Engraving and Printing.

The $1 Lincoln Memorial stamp was originally issued in Washington, D.C., and Springfield, Illinois, on February 12, 1923, the 114th anniversary of President Lincoln's birthday. The stamp features an engraving by Louis S. Schofield of the Bureau of Engraving and Printing.

The $2 U.S. Capitol stamp was first issued in Washington, D.C., on March 20, 1923. It features another engraving by Louis S. Schofield; this one is from a photograph of the East Front of the Capitol in the collection of the Bureau of Engraving and Printing.

The original $5 stamp was also issued in Washington, D.C., on March 20, 1923. Printed in two colors, the stamp features John Eissler's engraving of the head of "Freedom"—the magnificent statue by American sculptor Thomas Crawford that stands atop the Capitol dome. This stamp is a favorite of collectors, who sometimes refer to it as the "America."

ABOVE: The tower at the top of the Capitol dome.

FACING PAGE: The U.S. Capitol and the Lincoln Memorial are two sights enjoyed by philatelists.

WASHINGTON 2006
WORLD PHILATELIC EXHIBITION

The art of navigation from childhood has stimulated me to expose almost all my life to the impetuous waves of the ocean," declared Samuel de Champlain, "and has made me navigate and coast along a part of the lands of America, especially of New France." Jointly issued by Canada Post and the U.S. Postal Service, this stamp commemorates the 1606 voyage of Samuel de Champlain and recognizes the legacy of French exploration in North America.

A skilled cartographer, Champlain played a key role in French exploration of North America. In 1606, he accompanied lieutenant governor Jean de Biencourt de Poutrincourt on a mission to explore southward along the Atlantic coast. Beginning in Port Royal, in what is now Nova Scotia, the expedition reached as far south as modern-day Cape Cod. Remembered as a remarkable draftsman, Champlain created highly detailed maps and drawings and wrote numerous accounts of his travels, including descriptions of his encounters with local tribes. His works document the cultures and geography of the east coast of North America during the early 17th

The 1606 Voyage of Samuel de Champlain

century, and his maps are considered the first scientific documents relating to Canada.

Closely involved with French interests in North America for three decades, Champlain is also credited with the founding of Québec in 1608. Later, he explored the lake that still bears his name and journeyed as far west as Lake Ontario and Georgian Bay, part of Lake Huron. The third in a series issued by Canada Post to celebrate French settlements and related explorations in Canada between 1604 and 1608, this stamp was also featured on a souvenir sheet designed by Terrence W. McCaffrey of the U.S.

Postal Service and issued to coincide with the Washington 2006 World Philatelic Exhibition.

While Champlain might not have foreseen his 400-year legacy, he of all men understood the importance of cartographic and navigational skill, with words that might have applied to the spirit of partnership embodied by this joint issuance. "This should be prized highly by every nation of the world," he wrote in a 1632 treatise, "on account of the great benefits and advantages that kingdoms and countries receive therefrom, however near or far removed they may be."

Distinguished American Diplomats

"The first responsibility of good government is to safeguard the security of the nation," wrote the legislators who drafted the Rogers Act, the 1924 legislation that created the modern Foreign Service. "The first line of defense in achieving this first objective . . . is our diplomatic corps and those who direct it and back it up in the Department of State."

Mindful of their responsibility, diplomats serve as the nation's representatives around the world, where they promote foreign policy, resolve disputes, and work to protect American citizens abroad. Representing the best of their profession, the six diplomats featured on these stamps are remembered for their contributions to international relations, not only as negotiators and administrators but also as trailblazers, shapers of policy, peacemakers, and humanitarians.

While serving as a diplomat in France during World War II, Hiram Bingham IV (1903–1988) defied U.S. policy by issuing visas that saved the lives of more than 2,000 Jews and other refugees. Since the discovery of his heroism, he has been posthumously honored for "constructive dissent."

Frances E. Willis (1899–1983) began her diplomatic career in 1927 and served with distinction, especially in Europe, until 1964. She was the first female Foreign Service Officer to rise through the ranks to become an ambassador and the first woman to be honored with the title of Career Ambassador.

A skilled troubleshooter, Robert D. Murphy (1894–1978) played a key role in facilitating the Allied invasion of North Africa during World War II. He served as the first postwar U.S. ambassador to Japan, and in 1956 he became one of the first diplomats to be named Career Ambassador.

The distinguished career of Clifton R. Wharton, Sr., (1899–1990) spanned nearly four decades. In addition to becoming the first black Foreign Service Officer, Wharton was the first black diplomat to lead an American delegation to a European country and to become an ambassador by rising through the ranks rather than by political appointment.

A renowned expert on the Soviet Union, Charles E. Bohlen (1904–1974) helped to shape foreign policy during World War II and the Cold War. He was present at key wartime meetings with the Soviets, he served as ambassador to Moscow during the 1950s, and he advised every U.S. president between 1943 and 1968.

Philip C. Habib (1920–1992) was renowned for his diplomacy in some of the world's most dangerous flash points. An authority on Southeast Asia, a peace negotiator in the Middle East, and a special envoy to Central America, Habib was awarded the Presidential Medal of Freedom in 1982.

With background art featuring a collage of visas, passport pages, and other ephemera associated with diplomacy, this souvenir sheet commemorates these public servants for the roles they played in shaping the 20th century—and for putting a human face on American statecraft.

Distinguished American Diplomats

Judy Garland

Songwriters naturally appreciate the singers who present their work best: the ones who have a way with melody and rhythm, who can communicate many dimensions of a song, and who have clear diction when singing the lyrics. So it's no surprise that songwriters loved Judy Garland. Even though many artists recorded his works, Irving Berlin said, "No one has ever sung my songs better than Judy Garland." He could have been speaking for many in his profession.

Garland's fellow performers loved her, too. They praise her naturalness and sincerity as well as her technical brilliance. Many of her peers admired the quality of her concentration; they report that she could learn a lyric or the steps of a dance number with astonishing quickness. "Judy's the greatest entertainer who ever lived," said Fred Astaire, and many contemporary singers—Bette Midler, Audra McDonald, and Cyndi Lauper among them—call themselves Judy's fans, too.

Ray Bolger and Jack Haley co-starred with Garland in the 1939 classic *The Wizard of Oz.*

Her innate gifts as a performer and long experience—she made her professional debut at the age of two—put Garland in control of many tricks of the trade. "I learned something from watching Judy Garland," said Tony Bennett. "She knew the secret: a performer is a mirror. . . . You give to the audience, and that's what an audience will give back. Judy did that better than anyone else."

Composer Harold Arlen, who wrote the music for Garland's most popular movies—*The Wizard of Oz* and *A Star Is Born* among them—described her as "a treasure" and summed up his attitude with a suggestion: "Just give her a stage and a spotlight and get out of the way."

In essence, that was the approach taken to the Judy Garland stamp pane by art director Ethel Kessler and portrait artist Tim O'Brien. Designing the stamp was the dream of a lifetime for Kessler, who says she has "always been a Garland fan." She knew going in to the project that she wanted the stamp pane to show different aspects of Judy's lengthy and varied career. Working with O'Brien, she explored various combinations of images showing Garland

FACING PAGE: Garland was renowned for her brilliant concert performances.

This album of performances from Garland's Emmy-nominated television show was released in 1964.

as a film star with scenes of her performing in concert, mixing early film performances with later roles.

The list of possible combinations was endless. Garland was an all-around performer who appeared in 32 feature films, including both comedies and dramas. She was a best selling recording artist who released more than a dozen albums, nearly 100 singles, and made hundreds of radio broadcasts. She starred in 30 of her own television shows and made guest appearances on almost as many others. Her live performances, regarded as her supreme showcase, broke box office records. Garland could move audiences to tears; some of her admirers felt that in concert she erased the line between popular and high art.

Only sixteen years old at the time she filmed *The Wizard of Oz*, Garland won lasting international fame as Dorothy, the girl who rides a tornado from her home in Kansas to a land over the rainbow. From the beginning, Kessler thought that the image of Garland as Dorothy was key to the design.

After an image of Dorothy was chosen for the selvage, the question became which image to use for the stamp art. The design team agreed that Garland should look both stunningly beautiful and more mature than she did as an ingénue. Kessler and O'Brien tried hundreds of different combinations but kept coming back to a publicity shot from the 1954 film *A Star Is Born*. O'Brien used this photo as reference while painting his stamp portrait because he and Kessler felt it was the image that best captured the "star of stars" quality that made Judy famous.

LEFT: For her role in the 1954 film *A Star Is Born*, Garland received an Academy Award nomination.

RIGHT: Garland in the spotlight in *I Could Go On Singing*.

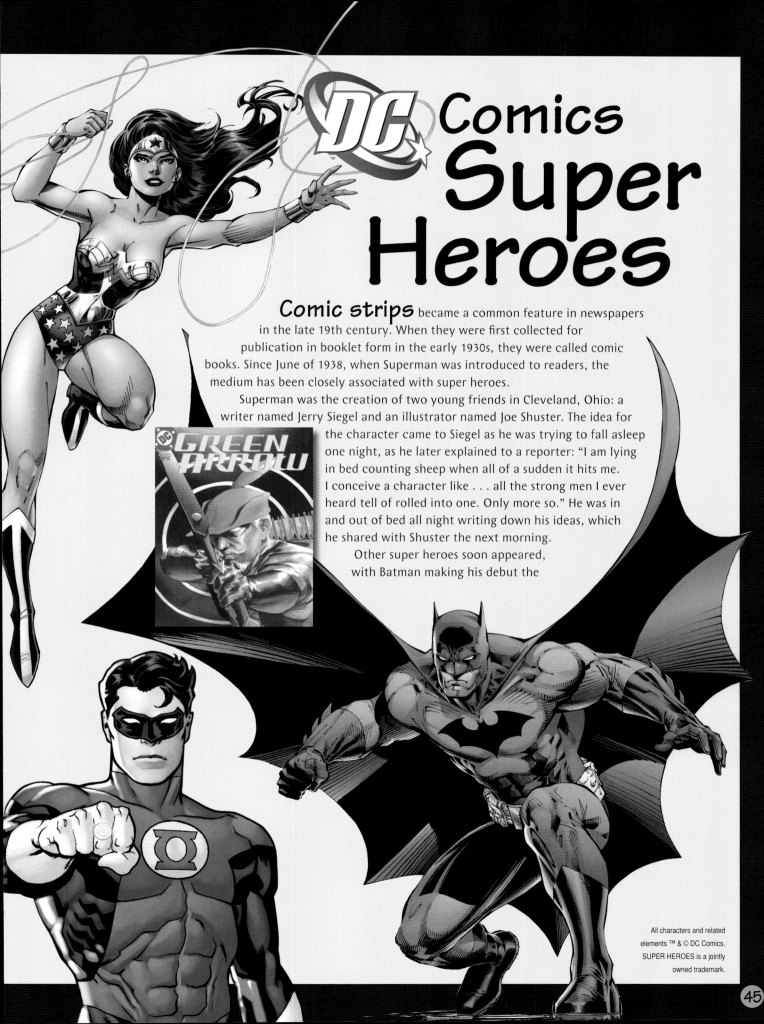

DC Comics Super Heroes

Comic strips became a common feature in newspapers in the late 19th century. When they were first collected for publication in booklet form in the early 1930s, they were called comic books. Since June of 1938, when Superman was introduced to readers, the medium has been closely associated with super heroes.

Superman was the creation of two young friends in Cleveland, Ohio: a writer named Jerry Siegel and an illustrator named Joe Shuster. The idea for the character came to Siegel as he was trying to fall asleep one night, as he later explained to a reporter: "I am lying in bed counting sheep when all of a sudden it hits me. I conceive a character like . . . all the strong men I ever heard tell of rolled into one. Only more so." He was in and out of bed all night writing down his ideas, which he shared with Shuster the next morning.

Other super heroes soon appeared, with Batman making his debut the

following year. Super heroes have responded to social and political issues from the start, becoming patriotic defenders of national interests, for example, during World War II. The war years were the peak of the so-called "Golden Age" of comic books, which were often included in care packages sent to members of the armed forces.

Comic books aren't simply kid stuff—adults have always been among their readers, and the form has attracted its share of serious artists. One of these, the noted cartoonist and writer Jules Feiffer, remembers entering the profession during the Golden Age: "We thought of ourselves the way the men who began movies must have."

Today, in the movies and on the page, super heroes thrill new and old fans alike.

Ott

Greenberg

Campanella

Mantle

Baseball Sluggers

Baseball fans always remember the sluggers: those power-hitters who wowed fans with awesome and often record-breaking home runs. This year, the Postal Service commemorates sluggers on stamps, honoring four versatile baseball players who set impressive standards for later generations.

A famous switch-hitter, Mickey Mantle could hit, run, and catch. In 1956, he enjoyed one of the greatest seasons in baseball history, hitting 52 homers with 130 RBI and a .353 batting average to win the Triple Crown. Synonymous with the New York Yankees for nearly two decades, Mantle is still considered one of the greatest players ever to take the field.

After several seasons in the Negro Leagues, Roy Campanella began playing for the Brooklyn Dodgers in 1948, becoming the first black catcher in the Major Leagues. During his ten-year Major League career, he hit 242 home runs, played as catcher in five World Series, and was named Most Valuable Player three times.

Hank Greenberg, considered one of the best right-handed batters of all time and baseball's first Jewish superstar, joined the Detroit Tigers in 1930. With 58 home runs in 1938, Greenberg tied Jimmie Foxx's home-run record for right-handed hitters, and his 11 multi-homer games set a one-season record that still stands.

Slugger Mel Ott generated more power with his unusual left-handed, high-stepping batting technique than the league had ever seen before. Distinguishing himself with the New York Giants for 22 seasons, Ott was the first National League player to hit 500 home runs, and he led the league in home runs six times.

Designed by Phil Jordan, these stamps capture the timeless nostalgia of the great American pastime. The four portraits by illustrator Lonnie Busch recall the trading cards from the period when baseball players were larger than life—national heroes who embodied the best of America.

Background: Fans pack the Polo Grounds for the final game of the 1923 World Series.

The Art of Disney
Romance

When designers from the U.S. Postal Service and Disney discussed concepts for the Art of Disney stamps, they considered how the mail helps friends stay in touch by marking special occasions with letters and cards. For this issuance, which highlights the theme of Romance, the design team noted that the mail can even keep true love alive across long distances. These new stamps remind us that true love is a wish that every heart makes—and that Disney characters embody our joy when we find our soul mates and expect that a bright future has begun.

The romance of Mickey Mouse and Minnie Mouse is probably the longest love affair in Disney history. Ever since he was introduced in *Steamboat Willie* in 1928, Mickey has captivated Minnie with his musical abilities. He may have ended up in trouble with Captain Pete, but he did win the girl; and Minnie stuck with Mickey and his dog, Pluto, through 73 cartoons. Even after all these years, Minnie still coos, "Aren't you sweet?"

For Cinderella and Prince Charming, the course of love did not always run smooth. Captured in the stamp art in the happily-ever-after, Cinderella made her big-screen debut in Disney's first full-length animated feature after World War II. It was a gamble for the studio, but fortunately, the public loved this retelling of the rags-to-riches fairy tale, making *Cinderella* one of the most successful films of 1950 and one of the most beloved animated classics of all time.

In 1955, *Lady and the Tramp* took another approach to the theme of romance. A classic romantic comedy, this love story about star-crossed lovers overcoming a series of obstacles tells the tale of a pampered cocker spaniel and a stray. Their first date, especially their memorable kiss over a plate of spaghetti, made the film one of the most romantic movies of its time.

Only true love could see past the mane of a lion, the head of a buffalo, the tusks of a wild boar, the brow of a gorilla, the legs of a wolf, and the body of a bear to see the man inside, but that's what happens in *Beauty and the Beast*. The film, which won accolades as one of the most delightful love stories ever told, was a labor of love on the part of nearly 600 artists, technicians, and animators. Many of them studied French painters to give the film its special ambiance—and to continue to honor the timeless theme of romance as only Disney can.

Disney Materials © Disney

Indian 1940 · 39 USA

Cleveland 1918 · 39 USA

Chopper c.1970 · 39 USA

Harley-Davidson 1965 · 39 USA

Motorcycles

Stamp artist Steve Buchanan is renowned for his award-winning work on such recent commemoratives as Reptiles and Amphibians, Carnivorous Plants, and Insects and Spiders. With this new issuance, he turns his digital-illustration techniques to machines, using restored motorcycles, reference photographs, and suggestions from owners and experts to create four stamps that honor the role of motorcycles in American culture.

Both lightweight and affordable, the single-cylinder 1918 Cleveland motorcycle was a popular bike of its day. With its 2.5-horsepower motor, it could, advertisements claimed, reach speeds of up to 35 to 40 miles per hour and travel 75 miles on a single gallon of gas. "A collector who served as our consultant really rides this motorcycle," Buchanan points out, "but we added the original tires with red sidewalls, and we even show the original compression-release lever, which the restored bike lacks."

To depict the 1940 Indian, an entry in a series of deluxe, four-cylinder motorcycles known as the Four, Buchanan worked with reference photos of a meticulously restored bike owned by a collector in New York City. "Like the Cleveland, the Indian artwork is based on a real bike, too," he says, "although we chose to show a different paint job in order to diversify the colors on the stamp pane." Depicted in the deep red often associated with Indian motorcycles, this streamlined bike features skirted fenders that partially cover the wheels, a

The 1969 film *Easy Rider* quickly brought choppers to the forefront of American culture.

controversial design innovation that soon became an Indian trademark.

With its whitewall tires, extensive chrome, large fenders, and fiberglass saddlebags, the Harley-Davidson featured on these stamps is considered one of the company's most iconic motorcycles. Known as the Electra-Glide, this model was first manufactured in 1965, when its new features included a push-button electric starter. To create a fitting portrait of this famous motorcycle, Buchanan enhanced its reflective surfaces. "I've created new reflections on all the chrome parts to be sure their shapes are clear in a tiny image," he says, "and I've provided some light in the engine details that typically just appear murky in photos."

In the case of the chopper featured on these stamps, Buchanan found even greater room for creativity. "We consulted with professional chopper builders, who helped us choose distinctive and accurate features such as the flame paint job," he explains. "The art represents a historic type of motorcycle from the imagination of the design team; it doesn't show a specific bike that actually existed."

Buchanan says many people frequently comment that his work looks "photographic," but he hopes his digital illustrations can accomplish something that photography cannot. "I'm trying to paint a description of what these objects are like," he says. "It may be comparable to what good portrait artists achieve, or what theatrical costumes and makeup accomplish. I'm hoping to make a picture that's so strongly descriptive that it will project even though the image scarcely fills a square inch."

Four competitive riders pause for a photo in San Diego around 1920.

Nature of America: Southern Florida Wetland

Florida's subtropical wetlands are remnants of a great wilderness that stretched unbroken for hundreds of miles until about a century ago. They still include some of the most extensive saw grass marshes and mangrove swamps in the world and support a remarkable number of tropical and temperate species. The eighth pane in the celebrated Nature of America series takes us to a southern Florida wetland—specifically, to an area where freshwater mingles with salt water along the coast, and where numerous kinds of plants and animals similarly mingle, as depicted by sharp-eyed artist John D. Dawson.

As Dawson's painting shows, a southern Florida wetland buzzes with life. Insects such as dragonflies and butterflies thrive there, along with hundreds of species of birds. Great egrets, wood storks, and numerous other wading birds feast on fish, frogs, and other small animals. Eagles hunt from the air, as do snail kites, an endangered species dependent on large, colorful apple snails. Cape Sable seaside sparrows, also extremely rare, weave nests a few inches above the ground and survive on seeds and insects.

The wetland supports numerous reptiles, including the American alligator and the American crocodile, which is found only in southernmost Florida—primarily in brackish and saltwater areas of the Everglades and Florida Keys. This stamp pane also includes one extremely rare mammal: the Florida panther, a long-tailed cat reaching more than six feet in length. It preys on deer and smaller animals found in cypress strands and other elevated areas. Another long-tailed mammal, the Everglades mink, inhabits freshwater shores and has a diet that includes birds, rodents, frogs, and fish.

In the southern Florida wetlands, a variety of trees, such as royal palms and West Indian mahoganies, flourish on natural rises known as hammocks. Often, their crowns filter sunlight and provide the indirect lighting favored by many flowers and other plants. More trees fringe coastal areas, especially in the southwest: Here, the exposed roots of salt-tolerant mangroves shelter marine organisms—and help stabilize the shores of this unique and fragile realm.

LEFT: A Florida panther emerges from the brush.

BACKGROUND: White ibis against a dramatic sky.

SOUTHERN FLORIDA WETLAND

NATURE OF AMERICA

EIGHTH IN A SERIES

Out of the bosom of the Air,
Out of the cloud-folds of her
　　garments shaken,
Over the woodlands brown and bare,
Over the harvest-fields forsaken,
Silent, and soft, and slow
Descends the snow.

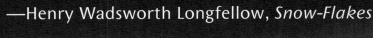

—Henry Wadsworth Longfellow, *Snow-Flakes*

Holiday Snowflakes

Longfellow was not alone in his fascination with snowflakes.

In 1885, Wilson Bentley of Jericho, Vermont, attached a microscope to his camera to take the first successful photographs of snow crystals. He dedicated his life to snowflake photography, capturing more than 2,000 snow crystal images.

Today, Kenneth Libbrecht continues Bentley's fascinating work. A professor of physics at the California Institute of Technology, Libbrecht studies snowflakes to satisfy his scientific curiosity about the material properties of ice and the elaborate patterns it develops. "Many materials form complex structures as they grow," he wrote in *The Snowflake: Winter's Secret Beauty*, "and in the case of snowflakes, we see the results falling from the sky by the billions."

Working quickly in the cold, Libbrecht uses a paintbrush to transfer snowflakes from cardboard to a glass slide. Placing the snowflakes into a temperature-regulated enclosure, he captures each image with a digital camera attached to a high-resolution microscope. For these stamps, he and art director Richard Sheaff selected two distinct snowflake patterns: stellar dendrites, which form branching treelike arms, and sectored plates, which, as their name suggests, form platelike arms.

For those of us in a festive mood, snowflakes offer a special form of winter art. With a magnifying glass and a cold surface, anyone can enjoy their elaborate patterns, shapes, and sizes. And, as Longfellow recognized, each snowfall has its own personality—so let it snow!

Christmas:

Chacón *Madonna and Child with Bird*

Spanish colonial art flourished in the New World between the mid-16th and early 19th centuries, especially in Mexico and Peru, where indigenous artists developed distinctive regional styles by combining native iconography with European artistic traditions. The painting on this new Christmas stamp, *Madonna and Child with Bird* by Ignacio Chacón, is imbued with the sacred symbols of two cultures, serving as a striking reminder of the diversity inherent in the spread of Christianity to the New World.

In Cuzco, the former capital of the Inca empire, Catholic churches were built over the ruins of Inca temples in an effort to promote the new religion among the indigenous people, and the city soon became the main art center in the Andes highlands. The mestizo-baroque style that emerged there in the mid-17th century came to be called the Cuzco School. Characterized by elements such as floral borders, vivid coloring, and *brocateado de oro*—gold-leaf overlay—the mestizo-baroque style became more elaborate over time and flourished during the late 17th and 18th centuries. One master painter of the Cuzco School, Marcos Zapata, was active from about 1748 to 1764, inspiring students and friends such as Ignacio Chacón to continue their personal interpretations of the mestizo-baroque style.

Particularly distinctive in the painting on this stamp is the small bird tethered by a red string. A famous painting by Spanish artist Bartolomé Esteban Murillo probably served as an indirect prototype for Chacón's painting, and the importance of birds in Inca culture would have made the topic of Murillo's painting particularly resonant in Peru. Birds were sacred to the Inca, partially because of their ability to fly and move closer to Inti, the sun god, and colonial artists in Cuzco often incorporated birds or feathers into images of the Virgin and Christ to indicate their divine status.

Dating to around 1765, *Madonna and Child with Bird* is part of the Engracia and Frank Barrows Freyer Collection of Peruvian colonial art at the Denver Art Museum. Brightly clothed figures rendered in exquisite detail against a dark background make this stamp a unique entry in a series that continues to please its devoted following.

CHRISTMAS

I. Chacón   Denver Art Museum

BACKGROUND: *Adoration of the Shepherds* by Bartolomé Esteban Murillo, an artist from 17th-century Spain.

Photo Credits

COVER, HALF TITLE, TITLE, FRONT MATTER, INTRODUCTION, CREDITS, and ACKNOWLEDGMENTS
Artwork courtesy DC Comics. All characters and related elements ™ & © DC Comics.

BLACK HERITAGE: HATTIE MCDANIEL
Page 8: Courtesy University of Southern California, Special Collections
Pages 8–9: GONE WITH THE WIND—Vivien Leigh and Hattie McDaniel. © Turner Entertainment Co. A Warner Bros. Entertainment Company. All rights reserved. Photo courtesy MPTV.net

LOVE: TRUE BLUE AND OUR WEDDING
Pages 10–11: Jupiter Images/Brand X Pictures

2006 OLYMPIC WINTER GAMES
Page 12: Agence Zoom/Getty Images

FAVORITE CHILDREN'S BOOK ANIMALS
Page 14: Wilbur from *Charlotte's Web* Illustration © renewed 1980 Estate of Garth Williams. Used with permission.
Page 14: Maisy™ © 2006 Lucy Cousins. Published by Candlewick Press, Cambridge, MA
Pages 14–15: The Very Hungry Caterpillar™ Eric Carle
Page 15: Dr. Seuss Properties ™ & © 2006 Dr. Seuss Enterprises, L.P.
Page 16: Frederick © 1967, 1995 Leo Lionni. Used with permission of Random House Children's books, a division of Random House, Inc.
Page 16: Olivia © 2005 by Ian Falconer
Pages 16–17: Where the Wild Things Are™ & © Maurice Sendak
Page 17: Curious George™ & © HMCo.

AMERICAN TREASURES: QUILTS OF GEE'S BEND
Pages 18–19: Photograph attributed to Edith Morgan, Courtesy of Tinwood Alliance

SUGAR RAY ROBINSON
Page 20 (Clockwise from top left): Time & Life Pictures/Getty Images
Page 21: © Bettmann/CORBIS

AMBER ALERT
Page 22: Artwork © Vivienne Flesher

LITERARY ARTS: KATHERINE ANNE PORTER
Page 24 (top and bottom): Papers of Katherine Anne Porter: Special Collections, University of Maryland Libraries
Pages 24–25: Photograph by George Platt Lynes © Estate of George Platt Lynes

BENJAMIN FRANKLIN
Page 26: National Portrait Gallery, Smithsonian Institution; Gift of the Morris and Gwendolyn Cafritz Foundation
Page 27: Courtesy National Archives, Washington, D.C.
Pages 28–29 (Background): Courtesy National Archives, Washington, D.C., Artwork © U.S. Postal Service

WONDERS OF AMERICA
Page 30: © Tom Bean/CORBIS
Pages 30–31: © Ron Watts/CORBIS; (Background): © Bettmann/CORBIS
Page 32 (Clockwise from left): © Galen Rowell/CORBIS; © George H. H. Huey/CORBIS; © Galen Rowell/CORBIS

WONDERS OF AMERICA (continued)
Pages 32–33 (Background): © Bettmann/CORBIS

Page 33 (Clockwise from top): © Phil Schermeister/CORBIS; © Royalty-Free/CORBIS; © Layne Kennedy/CORBIS; © Brett Baunton

WASHINGTON 2006: WORLD PHILATELIC EXHIBITION
Page 34 (Top): © Catherine Karnow/CORBIS, **(Background)** © Ron Watts/CORBIS

Page 35: Courtesy Architect of the Capitol, Washington, D.C.

THE 1606 VOYAGE OF SAMUEL DE CHAMPLAIN
Page 36: © Neil Rabinowitz/CORBIS

Pages 36–37: Courtesy Library of Congress, Washington, D.C.

DISTINGUISHED AMERICAN DIPLOMATS
Pages 38–39: © Joseph Sohm/CORBIS

Page 39: © Royalty-Free/CORBIS

LEGENDS OF HOLLYWOOD: JUDY GARLAND
Page 40: THE WIZARD OF OZ—Still of Judy Garland as "Dorothy" with the "Tin Man" and "Scarecrow." © Turner Entertainment Co. A Warner Bros. Entertainment Company. All Rights Reserved. Photopraph courtesy MPTV.net.

Pages 40-41: © Hulton-Deutsch Collection/CORBIS

Page 42 (top): Album cover courtesy of Capitol Records; **(bottom):** Photograph courtesy Photofest. A STAR IS BORN—Still of Judy Garland. © Warner Bros. Pictures, Inc. All Rights Reserved.

Page 43: I Could Go On Singing © 1963 Millar-Turman Productions, Inc. All Rights Reserved. Photopraph provided by John Fricke.

DC COMICS SUPER HEROES
Pages 44–47: Artwork courtesy DC Comics. All characters and related elements ™ & © DC Comics. Super Heroes is a jointly owned trademark.

BASEBALL SLUGGERS
Pages 48–49: All photographs © Bettmann/CORBIS

THE ART OF DISNEY: ROMANCE
Pages 50–51: Artwork courtesy Disney. Disney Materials © Disney

AMERICAN MOTORCYCLES
Pages 52–53: EASY RIDER © 1969, renewed 1997 Columbia Pictures Industries, Inc. All Rights Reserved. Courtesy Columbia Pictures. Photograph courtesy Photofest.

Pages 54–55: Courtesy San Diego Historical Society Research Library & Photograph Archives

Pages 54 (inset): © Leif Skoogfors/CORBIS

Pages 55 (inset): © Jack Fields/CORBIS

NATURE OF AMERICA: SOUTHERN FLORIDA WETLAND
Page 56 (left): Barbara Magnuson/Larry Kimball

Pages 56–57: Mark Barrett/Silver Image

HOLIDAY SNOWFLAKES
Page 58: © Kenneth G. Libbrecht

Pages 58–59: © Raymond Gehman/CORBIS

CHRISTMAS: CHACÓN *Madonna and Child with Bird*
Page 60: Photograph © Gianni Dagli Orti/CORBIS

Acknowledgments

These stamps and this stamp-collecting book were produced by Stamp Services, Government Relations, United States Postal Service.

JOHN E. POTTER
Postmaster General, Chief Executive Officer

THOMAS G. DAY
Senior Vice President, Government Relations

DAVID E. FAILOR
Executive Director, Stamp Services

Special thanks are extended to the following individuals for their contributions to the production of this book:

UNITED STATES POSTAL SERVICE

TERRENCE W. McCAFFREY
Manager, Stamp Development

CINDY L. TACKETT
Manager, Stamp Products and Exhibitions

SONJA D. EDISON
Project Manager

HARPERCOLLINS PUBLISHERS

KNOX HUSTON
Assistant Editor

LUCY ALBANESE
Design Director, General Books Group

SUSAN KOSKO
Production Director, General Books Group

HELEN SONG
Senior Production Editor

NIGHT & DAY DESIGN

TIMOTHY SHANER
Art Director, Designer

PHOTOASSIST, INC.

JEFF SYPECK
GREG VARNER
Editorial Consultants

MICHAEL OWENS
Photo Editor
Rights and Permissions

SARAH HANDWERGER
Rights and Permissions

REBECCA HIRSCH
Photo Research

JENNY TRUCANO
Traffic Coordinator
Photo Research

CRISTEN WILLS
Traffic

THE CITIZENS' STAMP ADVISORY COMMITTEE

CARY R. BRICK
MICHAEL R. BROCK
DAVID L. EYNON
JEAN PICKER FIRSTENBERG
HENRY LOUIS GATES, JR.
SYLVIA HARRIS
I. MICHAEL HEYMAN
JOHN M. HOTCHNER
KARL MALDEN
JAMES MIHO
JOAN MONDALE
RICHARD F. PHELPS
RONALD A. ROBINSON
MARUCHI SANTANA